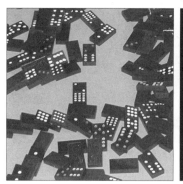

# CHAMPIONSHIP
# DOMINO
# TOPPLING

Robert Speca

# CHAMPIONSHIP DOMINO TOPPLING

Sterling Publishing Co., Inc.
New York

**The Speca Family: Mary Rose, Cheyenne, and Robert**

For more information about Robert Speca, Jr.
e-mail mmonroe@comcast.net or visit on website
www.dominoshow.com

*Illustrations by Robert Steimle*

**Library of Congress Cataloging-in-Publication Data Available**
Speca, Bob.
Championship domino toppling / Robert Speca.
     p. cm.
     Includes index.
     Rev. ed. of: The great falling domino book. c1979.
     ISBN 1-4027-1402-5
  1. Domino toppling—Juvenile literature. [1. Domino toppling.] I. Speca, Bob.
Great falling domino book. II. Title.
 GV1467.S63 2004
 795.32—dc22

                        2003025637


2  4  6  8  10  9  7  5  3  1


Published by Sterling Publishing Co., Inc.
387 Park Avenue South, New York, NY 10016
© 2004 by Robert Speca
Distributed in Canada by Sterling Publishing
c/o Canadian Manda Group, One Atlantic Avenue, Suite 105
Toronto, Ontario, Canada M6K 3E7
Distributed in Great Britain and Europe by Chris Lloyd at Orca Book
Services, Stanley House, Fleets Lane, Poole BH15 3AJ, England
Distributed in Australia by Capricorn Link (Australia) Pty. Ltd.
P.O. Box 704, Windsor, NSW 2756, Australia

*Manufactured in China*

Sterling ISBN 1-4027-1402-5

# Dedication

For my loving brother and best friend, Steve

Thanks

◧◨ *I must add a special thank you to the people who are most responsible for my successful domino career: my parents, Bob Speca, Sr., and Angel Speca. Their countless phone calls and hours spent in organization, public relations, and simply telling people about me at social gatherings sometimes go unacknowledged, but they are greatly appreciated. It's perfect having my parents as my managers, because they always make the decision that is best for me. They are also my biggest fans. I love them.*

*Thanks also to my agent Mark Monroe and everyone at Sterling Publishing Company for helping to put this book together.*

*Bobby*

# CONTENTS

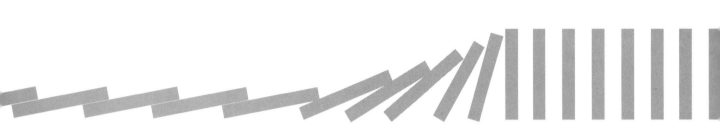

A toppling exhibition of 8,000 dominoes featuring a logo of Benjamin Franklin's kite (background) that was held in Philadelphia, PA on July 4, 2000.

# ||||| ˉINTRODUCTION

MANY years ago, at one of my many domino-toppling exhibitions, a youngster asked me in wide-eyed innocence how I got started in what he called "this crazy business." The question, a legitimate one, has undoubtedly remained unvoiced by many who believe that the pastime of setting up elaborate designs with dominoes, only to topple them, ranks right up there with goldfish-eating and flagpole-sitting.

Rather than defend domino-toppling, however, let me tell you how I got into this unusual calling. It might change your mind and convert you (as it did the youngster who asked the question) to the growing ranks of young-at-heart people who are pursuing the same pastime—one that may be the fastest growing hobby in America.

My childhood in Broomall, Pennsylvania, right outside Philadelphia, was largely indistinguishable from that of other kids my age. It was filled with utterly conventional pastimes: watching television; playing baseball, basketball, and football; and bicycling, swimming, and other fun-filled pursuits, up to and including falling in love with girls and cars. But not dominoes.

In fact, dominoes held absolutely no fascination for me. I considered the game to be at best boring, at worst a waste of time. That is, until my second year in high school. Till then, the only thing I associated with dominoes was the domino theory, a reference to one country in Southeast Asia falling to Communism and triggering a chain reaction throughout the whole area. Or something like that.

It was my second-year math teacher at Marple Newtown High who sparked my interest in domino-toppling. Mr. Dobransky asserted that the math induction principle we were then studying was analogous to having an infinite number of dominoes fall. (The math induction theory, for all of you who fell asleep in that class, is a deductive method of proof holding that if the first number in a proposition proves out, every other number in a long line of numbers will also prove out.) Mr. Dobransky told us that proving the first number in that long line was not unlike pushing over the first domino in a long line of dominoes. He said that if you had an infinite row of dominoes and they started toppling, they would never reach the end, even though they fall 100 times faster than they are set up.

I was intrigued enough by his theory to go out that very afternoon and buy four boxes of dominoes, the first I had ever owned. Hurrying home, I cleared a table in the den and lined up the contents of the four boxes—112 dominoes in all—in a straight line. Then I pushed over the first one and stood back. Sure enough, *click! click! click!,* they all fell down. Watching them fall was hypnotic. This was a sensation obviously shared by many others, because two years later Johnny Carson told me that when he had a set at home, he never played the game, he just knocked them over.

Still, it was all over in a couple of seconds—four seconds at the most. Surely, there had to be something more to it than this, I thought. Something more entertaining.

Thinking, *What if I were to set them up in an even longer line?* I went out and bought more, despite my parents' hints (in that time-honored manner for which parents are famous) that I was wasting my money.

As my ambitions grew, so did my collection of dominoes— at the rate of a box a day. No longer was the den table adequate, even with two leaves attached, as I tried to cram boxful after boxful of dominoes onto it. The quantum increase in dominoes forced me to seek a new surface. (That, and the fact that my mother wanted to repossess the den table and floor for family use. One wonders what the mother of young Thomas Edison did with *his* experiments!)

Relinquishing my claim on the den table, I moved my activities down to the basement. I found that the basement floor, while not the best of surfaces, at least didn't have any of the abnormal undulations caused by water that are often associated with basement floors. However, the family ping-pong table was in the basement, and, more often than not, my younger brother would smack his ball directly into one of my designs.

Although the basement floor was hardly the ideal surface for setting up long rows of dominoes, it did give me the area to try special effects like the letter S and circles. These led to short turns, like those in the letter S, that go back and forth; softer turns that look like waves in the ocean; and, finally, my very first design, the peace sign—which was merely a circle with three lines in the center.

All the while I was discovering, on an almost daily basis, more and more about my new hobby: that one domino could knock over two or three others; that dominoes could be aimed at other objects; that they could fall uphill; and that if dominoes could split off into two lines to ensure the continuation of the chain, they could split off into three or more. And many other effects.

Some of those effects were made possibly by my discovery of larger-sized dominoes. These two-inch dominoes not only provided versatility, but also ensured that certain patterns such as figure eights and other intersections wouldn't run into each other, going instead over the already fallen smaller dominoes.

(Once I went out in quest of 20 boxes of these larger-sized dominoes and, finding that all the local stores were out of stock, I bicycled seven miles to purchase them from a place cutesily called "Kiddie City.")

As my lines and designs developed, my only audience was my parents, who helped me set up on occasion. I had never really "performed." Still, I thought that toppling dominoes might appeal to others. Finally, the opportunity to unveil my skills came one day during my junior year in high school. I invited a couple of friends over and proceeded to set up some 500 dominoes in a half hour and topple them over. Their oohs and aahs confirmed my hope that domino-toppling would appeal to others besides my family. Two weeks later, they asked me, "Hey, when are you going to do those dominoes again?"

From that time on, my after-school activities became one long period of Show and Tell as I lined up dominoes in various formations for an ever-increasing audience, even inviting them to participate by hitting the first domino to start the chain. Classmates soon began coming over to watch the dominoes fall, almost as if it were a regularly scheduled extra-curricular activity. I probably could have charged admission. But their excitement was enough of a reward.

My friends, too, got caught up in the excitement of watching the dominoes falling over at the rate of about 30 to 35 a second. Soon they were throwing out ideas: "Have two lines at one time," "Have them race each other," and "Why not have the dominoes go this way?" It became a community project as I began incorporating their ideas into my patterns.

Not long thereafter, the local newspaper, the *County Leader*, took notice of the goings-on in my basement and gave me my first write-up, putting me on the front page right up there with the stories on potholes. A few weeks later the *Philadelphia Bulletin* devoted a pictorial spread in its Sunday magazine to my domino-toppling, and I became known as the Domino Wizard.

The publicity fanned the curiosity of friends and acquaintances, and they began to descend on my basement in numbers that easily rivaled the attendance at Friday football games. By this time, I had hit upon the technique of setting up the dominoes before "show time." That way, I was able to commence the daily show immediately upon the audience's arrival, instead of having them wait for an hour while I set up 1,000 dominoes. In front of these appreciative audiences, I tried out different "highlights" like letters, ramps, intersections, flags, and other esoteric designs.

Once someone in the back of the room suggested, "Hey, maybe you can get on TV!" meaning the local news station.

Robert Speca's first big toppling feat of 5,555 dominoes was captured in his family's basement by *The County Leader* newspaper in 1974.

Although this didn't work out, I did get on a local TV show hosted by Al Alberts, a member of the singing group called the Four Aces, which had turned out hit after hit during the 1950s, including "Tell Me Why" and "Garden in the Rain." Later, with a line of dominoes approaching 5,000 in number and extending into all four corners of the basement, my friend Bill Passman asked aloud, "I wonder if that's the largest chain in the world? You should write to Guinness and they'd probably put it in the world records."

That, too, seemed like a good idea. And so, investing another $2.50 in my hobby, I went out and bought the latest edition of *The Guinness Book of World Records* with the idea of finding out what the world record was. Surprisingly, there was no such listing. But as I thumbed through the book, I came across a page in the front that told me—or any other interested reader, for that matter, although I have always believed it was meant for my eyes alone—that I could create an entirely new category by merely filling out the blank and sending it in.

I tore out the page and sent it in with a note saying something inane like, "I have a bunch of dominoes and line them all up. Does that sound interesting enough to be included in your new book of world records?"

The Guinness people were quick to respond. They would consider including such a record in their next edition, they said, to be called "Dominoes toppled in a continuous chain from one hit," provided I could meet their verification standards. Two people would have to sign notarized statements that they had actually seen the event take place, and I would have to provide Guinness with photographs of the event.

Meeting the standards sounded easy enough, but I had no

idea what the record would—or should—be. There was no such thing as a record for domino-toppling, no magic number to shoot at. I was left to my own devices.

I chose the number 11, not only because it was my lucky number, but also because I like things in multiples of 11. Therefore, my record would be 11,111 dominoes.

I went about setting up 11,111 dominoes in a massive configuration that sometimes took on the look of a jigsaw puzzle put together by drunken carpenters—here split-offs ending in highlights like the American flag; there intersections up to and including figure eights, Triple Intersections, DNA chains, peel-offs, ramps, and Ram's Horns; even a few wooden contraptions thrown in for good measure. And everywhere there were lines, letters, and long, sweeping curves. It was a fun design, if I do say so myself, and it required no less than 11 hours and 400 boxes to set up. It was a feat worthy of being the world's record.

Secure in the knowledge that I would be included in the 1976 edition of *The Guinness Book of World Records*, I indulged in one of my lifelong fantasies by writing to *The Tonight Show* in an attempt to get on. Surprise of surprises, they told me they'd like to have me on the show sometime that spring.

It was a dream come true. Here I was, a high school senior, invited out to Los Angeles to appear on the second-longest-running show on television with an act that had rarely been seen outside my basement. I felt like an impostor. But regardless of my shortcomings, there was one thing I longed for: to be known by everyone as the best in my field, by the nickname my high school classmates had given me, the Domino Wizard.

My trip to California was no different from that of any kid

traveling with his parents, his younger brother, and 20 cases of dominoes stored somewhere in the plane's hold for his first appearance on national television. From the moment I stepped off the plane, I found California to be just as it had been depicted: sunny, smoggy, and showy. I loved it. Almost as soon as we checked into our hotel, I saw celebrities who had been known to me only through magazines or the 23-inch screen in my living room, people like Tony Randall, Peter Falk, and Robert Blake. It was as far removed from anything I had ever done before as my basement in Broomall was from the studio in Universal City. But somehow it was happening to me! It was exciting and scary. I was more concerned with what I was going to say during the interview than with the patterns I would be setting up.

The producers of *The Tonight Show* put me at ease. Not only were they understanding of the problems a novice like me faced, but they, too, were eager to make my segment of the show a success—both for them and for me. They indicated that they'd do their damnedest to get anything I needed.

What I needed most was to know the actual time they had allocated for my "act." It was one of the four elements I had to know in order to set up and perform properly. Once they told me that my portion of the show would be three and a half minutes, I was able to figure out the number of dominoes, the area, and the length of time I needed to set up. For three and a half minutes of dominoes falling at the rate of 30 per second—give or take a few seconds, since dominoes falling on a curve go down faster because they're set up closer to ensure they will hit one another—I figured I'd need approximately 7,000 dominoes, which would take about 35 square yards, at the rate of 5 square yards per 1,000. That meant a setup time of about seven hours.

I started setting up in the studio at 9 A.M., and even with a few tricky uphill ramps, an intersection, and Johnny Carson's name spelled out—plus a few "firebreaks," or voids where I took the precaution of leaving out a couple of dominoes until the time of the show, just in case one of them fell over prematurely—I finished five and a half hours later, in time for the early taping.

After having makeup applied to ensure the right facial tones (whatever that means), I sat backstage in the greenroom with the other guests, including comedienne Joan Rivers, and awaited my national television debut. We could hear the audience coming into the studio and the "warm-up" announcer's welcoming remarks to prime them for their part in *The Tonight Show*, followed by a disembodied voice hollering out "Stand by" and some numbers being counted down. Then, Doc Severinsen's band struck up the show's theme and I heard an announcer saying something like "… and Bob Speca, the Domino Wizard." This was it!

As I waited through the introduction by Ed McMahon, Johnny Carson's opening monologue, and the first commercial break, all my mental preparation, and makeup, seemed to drain away. I could feel butterflies in my stomach, and my palms were sweaty. After what seemed like an eternity, I was finally brought to my waiting place behind the curtains by an assistant director. Then, in what might have been a dream, I heard my name, and the curtains were pulled back to allow me to enter, stage right. Here I was, Bob Speca of Broomall, Pennsylvania, on *The Tonight Show* with Johnny Carson!

Johnny did his best to put me at ease, talking about my world record of 11,111 dominoes and mentioning that he, too, as a kid, had knocked over dominoes. Then it was up to me to "do my thing." As I went over to topple the first domino, I could only think, *What if it doesn't work?* But the fates—and the physics of momentum—were with me. Row after row of dominoes, including Johnny's name, fell down on schedule. It was a success! So much of a success, in fact, that they repeated the show three more times as part of the Johnny Carson "Anniversary Show."

That was the good news. The bad news was that several students in Seattle saw me on *The Tonight Show* and heard me tell Johnny that my record was 11,111 dominoes. That apparently gave them something to shoot for, and before I knew it, I was the ex-Guinness record holder. The 1976 edition included their new record of 13,832.

Well, it was back to the drawing board. So when I appeared on *David Frost Presents the Guinness Book of World Records*, I built a 15,000-domino chain to ensure my claim at least for another year. I then constructed a pattern containing twice my former number of dominoes—22,222—in a special Bicentennial design that took me nineteen hours to set up. That was good enough to get me into the 1977 Guinness record book.

By now the game of one-upmanship had become international. An Englishman built a continuous chain of 33,000. I later set up 50,000 at my dorm, Hill House, at the University of Pennsylvania, and then 55,555 at the Palestra on the Penn campus.

With the world's record secured for at least another year, I put my hobby-*cum*-profession to practical use. I had enrolled at the University of Pennsylvania, where I was majoring in astronomy and, as any college kid can tell you, could use all the money I could get my hands on to help my dad underwrite

the costs. I appeared on *The Tony Orlando Show*, at the special premiere for the Goldie Hawn and Chevy Chase movie *Foul Play*, and on *The Tonight Show* again. In addition to those trips to the Coast and my classes—not to mention being on the swim team—I also put in appearances at shopping centers and made commercials in cities such as Minneapolis, Dallas, San Francisco, Milwaukee, and Toronto. Not only was it fun, it was lucrative.

But perhaps the most satisfying moment I experienced was one that wasn't lucrative, merely fun—and worthwhile. In 1978, I donated my time and skills to the National Hemophilia Foundation to set up a 100,000-long chain of dominoes at the Manhattan Center in New York City: my first appearance there. After lugging sixty large crates of dominoes to New York—including several I had painted red, white, and blue for the flag effect—I found what was, at best, an uneven floor. After I had put in over eleven days setting up the dominoes,

Robert Speca relaxing after setting the World Record for domino-toppling in 1976, knocking down 22,222.

leaving firebreaks between rows to ensure they wouldn't topple over because of drafts, I reentered the next day to find little areas where the dominoes had fallen, courtesy of either poltergeists or cockroaches.

With the New York press, Guinness representatives, and National Hemophilia officials in attendance, I pushed the first of the 100,000 dominoes and stood back proudly as they went merrily on their way—clicking off a new world's record. Everything went as planned. The lines, the ramps, the flag, the letters spelling out "National Hemophilia Foundation," and intersections all fell down on schedule. But then an ABC cameraman leaned far over the balcony to take a shot of the quickly moving design. And before you could say "Click!" a little press card fluttered out of his pocket onto the floor, striking a standing domino and starting its own independent chain reaction.

I froze in disbelief as the finale of my act happened without me—balloons exploding and mousetraps popping—but it turned out all right. The Guinness people rushed out onto the floor and verified that 97,500 dominoes had toppled, a new world record, and that the cameraman, Manny Alpert, had knocked over only 2,500. Relieved by that news, I gave Mr. Alpert his own domino as a memento of the event, and then proceeded to scoop up all 100,000 tiles, which I had by now begun to call "those little devils," back into their cartons for the long trip home.

With the goal of toppling 100,000 dominoes accomplished, I conceived the ultimate ambition of setting up 1,111,111 dominoes on a football field in a sort of Domino Spectacular, complete with every design known to man—and then some—

and charging people $11.11 to watch the six hours of falling dominoes that would take me almost two months to set up. Unfortunately, the cost of renting space for this event proved prohibitive. However, in 1981, I set up 111,111 dominoes in Denver, my largest topple to date.

My 30 years of experience with dominoes has granted me access to venues that would never have been possible otherwise. I have appeared on the TV shows *That's Incredible* (twice), *On the Road With Charles Kuralt*, *The Super Dave Osborne Show*, *The Arsenio Hall Show*, *Mr. Rogers' Neighborhood*, *Reading Rainbow*, and *The Ellen DeGeneres Show*. I have also done countless setups for local entertainment venues, TV commercials, and private and commercial films, including *The Toy* with

Robert Speca setting up a unique exhibition featuring the toppling of 10,000 Nintendo cartridges in Chicago in 1996.

Thirty years of experience with dominoes has allowed the author to meet many celebrities, including his favorite rock band Kansas, Mr. Rogers, and actor Jamie Kennedy. *Top photo courtesy of Image Maker Photography and Video. Bottom left photo courtesy of Impact Multi Image.*

Jackie Gleason and Richard Pryor. I have set up dominoes on the Great Wall of China, and celebrated Tom Monaghan's (Domino's Pizza tycoon) 60th birthday with an intricate setup.

Many of the celebrities I have met impressed me, for different reasons. Charles Kuralt seemed much more interested in the science and artwork behind the design than the number of dominoes. Fred Rogers had a very professional and relaxed manner, even during stressful and busy shooting schedules. He spoke to me the same way he spoke to the children on his show, except he used bigger words. I can't remember laughing so hard as with Super Dave Osborne (aka Bob Einstein).

Rehearsal was so funny that I could barely keep a straight face during the actual taping. (As an aside, most of the interviewers were good at keeping me relaxed. Although some interviews were scripted, the best ones occurred when the interviewer and I briefly discussed domino-toppling before the show, and the conversation was allowed to flow freely during the actual interview.)

My success at domino-toppling and all my other accomplishments would not have been possible without the discipline and desire instilled in me by my parents and teachers. This ability to focus has helped me through times when I had to reset thousands of dominoes in an hour after someone had knocked them down prematurely.

It is this discipline and desire that allowed me to graduate with a Bachelor's degree in astronomy from the University of Pennsylvania. I have gone on to teach high school science at Academy Park High School in Sharon Hill, Pennsylvania. These qualities also fueled my participation in road races and triathlons. I have competed in 14 Ironman triathlons (including the Double Ironman in Huntsville, Alabama), run 130 marathons (and have even completed the tortuous Western States 100 Mile Trail Run), and coached swimmers who have won Olympic gold medals. Domino-topping has instilled in me focus and concentration, attributes I have found invaluable as a lifeguard patrolling the Ocean City, New Jersey, beaches for 25 summers. It has also granted me the financial freedom to travel the world and see the band Kansas perform 100 times.

I am proud to say that I helped launch the domino-toppling craze that began over three decades ago and continues to this day. The world record, with unlimited people setting up dominoes, is presently over 4 million dominoes, as teams of more than 100 workers have coordinated their efforts for impressive massive setups in Europe and Asia. Perhaps you will be inspired by this book, and will attempt to better this record.

Carl Sagan is quoted as saying, "The universe is not required to be in perfect harmony with human ambition." Making the universe a more harmonious place for others is what I have strived to achieve through domino-toppling.

Life is good!

**An exhibition commemorating the 2004 graduating class of Academy Park High School, Sharon Hill, PA. Many of the domino-toppling exhibits shown here are discussed in the following pages.**

# ABOUT DOMINOS

DOMINOES are almost as old as playing cards, dating
back to ancient China. Apparently designed to represent
all the possible throws of two Chinese dice, the faces of the
small rectangular tiles are divided into halves, with each half
marked with spots (or "pips") similar to a pair of dice lying
side by side. Dominoes first appeared in Europe around the
middle of the eighteenth century, and were introduced into
England by French prisoners toward the end of the 1700s. The
name *dominoes* comes from the priest's coat, called a "domino." However, the European import differed from the Chinese
original in the number of tiles (or "bones") used in the game
(down from 32 to 28) and the addition of a blank tile.

Today, there are several variations of the game of dominoes, the most popular one being the Block Game, in which
the dominoes are shuffled, face down on the table, and five
to seven tiles are selected by each of two to four players. The
opening lead is made by the player drawing the highest
doublet, or the tile with the highest number of pips on it. Each
player, in turn, attempts to match his tile to the end
of the last played tile. (For example, if the opening lead is a
double-six, the next player must lay down a tile with six pips
on one end to the end of the tile just played.) This continues

until one player is out of those drawn, or neither of the two (or none of the four) players can make another move. Then the player who has gone "out" gets the total number of pips shown on the dominoes in the hands of those playing.

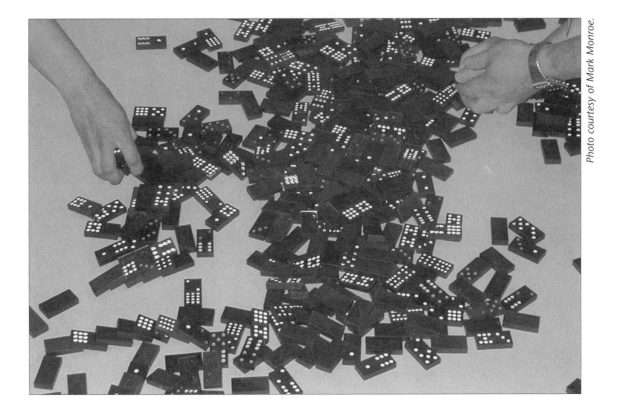

# BEGINNER DESIGNS

Beginner domino-toppling designs include straight lines and turns.

# Straight Lines

TOPPLING dominoes is easy. The hard part is setting them up so they can be toppled over. And the proper place to start is with a straight line, the most elementary formation.

Building straight lines is merely a matter of knowing how far apart to space the dominoes. Since most dominoes are about an inch and a half tall, you should space them an inch or less apart so that when they fall they strike the domino in front. If the distance between dominoes is more than an inch, they'll miss each other. Less than an inch is perfectly all right, provided they're not too close together, say a half-inch; then you'll find the dominoes fall too quickly and the anticipated effect will be ruined because too many will be hitting per second.

After some experimentation, you'll find you can gauge the distance. If you put a ruler down next to the dominoes, you'll probably find that your ability to judge distance is fairly accurate. After a few times, you'll never need that ruler again.

In setting up, make sure that each domino is a mirrored reflection of the one immediately in front of it—they should look like soldiers standing in a row. Don't have them facing every which way like a free-form art exhibition; that will not only decrease the chances of the one behind hitting the one in front, but it will also make it highly probable that one will fly out of line and knock over another line close by.

Try as many dominoes as you want in the beginning. When I first started, I would have as many as 112 in a straight row (four sets of dominoes), though I sometimes experienced difficulties. But before you try any fancy stuff, master the art of putting your dominoes in a straight line and having them fall over without a miscue. If you don't succeed the first time—or even the sixth—try, try again! A domino-toppler needs to develop patience in order to become a success.

One word of caution: The surface you select is essential to your success. Seek a flat, hard surface. Formica surfaces, cement floors, and, of course, basketball courts are perfect. Never attempt to set up your dominoes on a rug! If you do, you'll become frustrated before you have started to get the hang of this fascinating hobby.

Before going on to the next formation—or "trick"—there is one extension of the straight-line discipline you can try. Take the empty domino boxes, or any other empty boxes you may have around the house, and put them over the dominoes, making a little tunnel for the line to go through. This will not only provide a little suspense (because you won't be able to see the dominoes fall) but will also ensure that you've set up the dominoes at the right spacing and angle to fall in a straight line.

**Straight-line basics. The dominoes are lined up like soldiers standing in a row.**

# Turns

■■ TURNS are two straight lines that are connected in such a way that they go in different directions. The idea is to make the dominoes closer on the inside of the turn than on the outside. They should almost touch on the inside of the turn because less of the surface areas hits the next domino on a turn.

You'll discover more about domino turns through experience than from description. If you turn the dominoes in and the turn doesn't work, place them a little closer together on the inside the next time. Soon you'll find that you can turn your straight lines in any direction you want—90 degrees, 180 degrees, anything. But a word of caution: You don't want sharp turns, especially when 100,000 dominoes depend on one domino in a curve. In the basic turn, dominoes are spaced closer together on the inside of the turn than on the outside.

**In the basic turn, dominoes are spaced more closely on the inside of the turn than on the outside.**

# Split-Offs

■■ $S$PLIT-OFFS—dominoes going into two lines—are the key to most of the advanced formations. Split-offs allow more freedom in design and are necessary to the continuation of a setup in many instances.

The idea of a split-off is to have one domino hit two dominoes so that the pattern can branch off into two lines. Imagine those same soldiers that made up the straight line. But this time, instead of lining up directly behind one another, they have moved, ever so slightly, to a position where the narrow portions of their shoulders are almost touching, in an ever-broadening pattern.

As the introductory line—much like the bottom stem of the letter Y—comes up to the split-off, the last domino hits two others. The two lines branch out, going in different directions.

Split-offs hardly ever foul up. They are, in effect, a safety valve to ensure the success of the setup. Only once did a split-off not work for me—and even then, half of it did. That's the beauty of split-offs.

But split-offs are much more than safety valves. They are also designs in themselves. By combining the disciplines

**The basic split-off. The final domino in the stem strikes two closely positioned dominoes at the base of the fork and creates two falling lines.**

learned in making turns and creating split-offs, you can have two lines racing each other, curving around like a Grand Prix racing track or the letter S. This is called the Inside-Outside Loop and comes out of a split-off into two rows with the left line continuing to make an S-curve, and the right wavy line making another S alongside it—one inside, the other outside, and then changing over.

I sometimes have these two lines race each other for about 15 to 30 seconds. However, I wouldn't devote any more time to the Inside-Outside Loop—or even to two lines falling concurrently. Whereas 100 dominoes can take three seconds to fall in a straight line, a split-off of two rows falling simultaneously takes only one and a half seconds, thereby robbing you of half your show. And, just as importantly, it tends to distract the eye from other tricks and highlights going on elsewhere.

**The Inside-Outside Loop.**

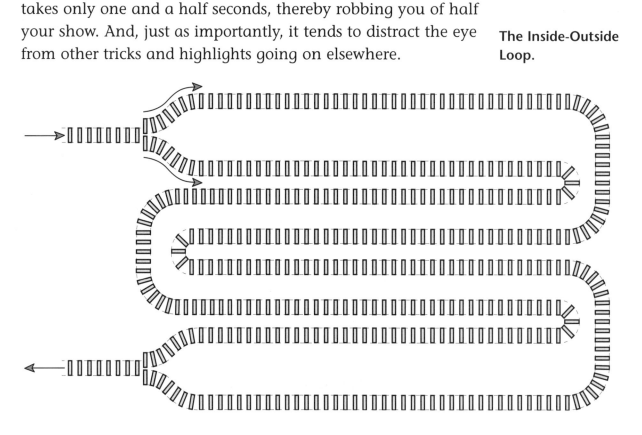

A 10,000-domino setup featuring an alphabet display. It reads "Sebastien C' est Fou!" (Sebastian is Crazy) for a French television show of that name that was popular in 1993.

# The Alphabet

◧▪ YOU can make virtually any letter in the alphabet—or any number—merely by mapping it out beforehand on the floor. The process is similar to tracing something on a piece of paper. Through experimentation, you will find that your letters, like your penmanship, improve in appearance, and just as you discarded the ruler to measure the one inch difference in the dominoes you set up in a straight line, you will soon be able to dispense with your precharted letters and numbers. With your eye alone, you will be able to connect the dominoes to form any letter you want, and eventually an intelligible word pattern.

Letters are virtually foolproof because they are an outgrowth of split-offs, all springing off a baseline (the main line, which continues the flow of the pattern) created to ensure the continuation of the pattern to the next letter.

Most letters are simple to do. Let's make the letter O. O stems up from one point on the baseline, the bottom splitting off onto the next letter. At the top of the line that is going to make the letter, the dominoes go into a very slow curve. If you want to plot it out, you can put one domino at each 90-degree point of the circle—say, at the 12 o'clock, 3 o'clock, 6 o'clock, and 9 o'clock positions—so that you know where you want to be at a certain point. Otherwise, your circle might not be symmetrical.

C, D, P, R, and U are all made using the same formula, with curves and split-offs. B is two turns with a middle bar. Coming

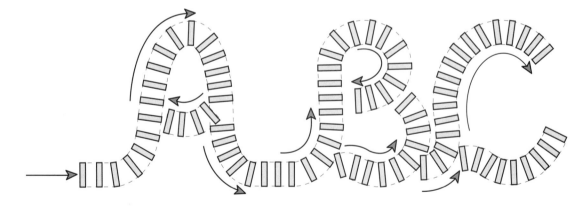

off the connecting baseline, you have a split-off with a straight line forming the spine of the letter B. Then, at the top—approximately nine inches tall—you make a turn to form the top of the B and start coming down in a gradual turn to form the middle of the letter. From there, you make another turn to reconnect with the baseline, which continues the chain to the remainder of the letters.

The letter T is made by a split-off from the baseline—one of the lines making a left turn up into the letter, the other continuing onto the next letter. The line that made the left turn goes up to form the base of the T, and then at the top of the stem there is yet another split-off, with one of the lines going to the left and the other to the right to form the cap of the letter. Both of these lines die off.

Certain letters are easy to construct and recognize. I, for example, is just a straight line going up, which can be dotted by putting a little circle at the top. The letter P is nice and centered, and the R is just P with an extra leg made by a split-off.

In order to make a recognizable W and M, you have to devote more space and make the letters really large. Otherwise, the split-offs tend to become crunched up at the bottom. These two, which I call full letters, should stem up from the baseline, and come back down. By experimentation, you will be able to make them readable.

Since W is a double V (or double U), it is basically V done

**The Domino Alphabet. As with penmanship, you'll find your letters improve with practice. F, K, M, Q, W, and X are the most difficult letters; A, F, H, K, M, N, and R have no baselines; M and W need extra space.**

twice and joined in the center, *without* a baseline between the two parts. M is not as hard, because the connecting points are at the bottom. (Similarly, A has two connecting points at the bottom—again, without a baseline between the two vertical legs of the letter—R has two, and T and I have one each.)

Certain letters are troublesome primarily because they look like other letters. The letter L, for instance, tends to look like the letter I, because the bottom of the letter commingles with the baseline. One way to distinguish the two is to dot the I. Another is to make a little lip, or upward curve, of two extra pieces at the end of the bottom of the L—giving it a script look. Still another way is to have the connecting line at the top of the letter instead of off the baseline.

Another letter that is somewhat confusing is Q, which looks like an O unless there's a little tail extending below the baseline. Because this requires the building of an intersection—something we won't come to until the Advanced Designs section—I suggest that at this point in your domino-toppling education you twist the tail.

It should be evident to all from the context of the word that the letter is a Q, especially since it is always followed by a U in the English language.

Perhaps the most confusing letter of all is F, because coming off the baseline it tends to look like an E. I usually have F come from the last letter, without a baseline. Thus, the top part of the F is an inverted baseline—or headline—that stems down, rather than up, into the next letter, which then comes down into the baseline. Another strategy is to spray-paint the dominoes used in the baseline the same color as the floor so that the black dominoes in the letter F stand out from the baseline. And, as with the letter L, a third way to differentiate the F is to give it a little tail on the top horizontal line, made up of a couple of dominoes.

For all the problems in building Fs, Ws, and Ms, the two most difficult characters to make are X and K. Both letters involve three or four split-offs within a two-square-inch area, and are hard to make look good unless you use smaller dominoes.

K is formed by having the right side of the split-off form two 45-degree legs of the letter. There are three connecting points, all coming together in the center to form the letter. Usually I put three dominoes together to guide me in building the legs, sometimes even making the right leg of the K look like an arch (or a script K) so that the turn is gradual. (Of course, this can also be done for the letter H.)

X is almost the same, except more difficult. Here, we have an introductory leg off the baseline going from the lower left-hand corner and meeting three others in the middle, making, in effect, four legs.

Both letters are time-consuming to make, but practice and patience will win out, and pretty soon you'll be able to build any letter and any word. And sometimes you'll even misspell a word as an attention-catching device!

You can now try entire words, even the name of girl- or boyfriends. It's like tattooing someone's name on your arm or writing it on a tree, only somewhat less permanent.

Years ago, I constructed entire slogans before the University of Pennsylvania swim team competed against one of its opponents, to psych up my teammates. And whether it was "GO PENN" or "IMPALE YALE" or "ROLL OVA VILLANOVA," the effect was the same: It was hypnotic and at the same time exciting, and was guaranteed to stir up emotions.

# INTERMEDIATE DESIGNS

# Ramps

ONCE you've become acquainted with—if not mastered—the Beginner's section, you can move on to the next level, the Intermediate designs.

The first design is called the Ramp. Its purpose is to elevate your dominoes to a position where they can be seen and break up the monotony of similar-type designs all over the floor. The underlying principle of ramps is that dominoes, like cars, will travel uphill.

I developed the principle of ramps out of boredom. I got tired of doing straight lines and thought there had to be something else. There was. It required a little ingenuity, and a yardstick.

Elevate your yardstick about two or three inches by placing one-half of one of your domino boxes underneath it at one end. You can brace the yardstick by anchoring the lower end with the other half of the box—thus providing yourself with a platform.

When you're sure the yardstick is secure and won't vibrate while you're placing your dominoes along its length, begin placing your dominoes slowly up the ramp. You can put as many as you want, up to 36, the number I usually place up the ramp. If they start falling, lower the angle of the yardstick. You'll soon find that dominoes will stay upright only with a yardstick angle of 10 degrees or lower.

After you've placed your dominoes so that they appear to be gradually climbing the yardstick, you can have the last one on the bridge either fall off and hit another domino on the floor under it, or die out and merge back into the split-off that started the whole chain up the yardstick.

Although theoretically the ramp works perfectly, it has failed me on more than one occasion. One time was with a rather intricate design I had set up for the *Mike Douglas Show*. Fortunately, the producer was able to edit out the mishap and the dominoes went merrily on their way on the TV screen. But I now use a split-off to ensure the continuation of my chain of dominoes.

There are many different types of ramps. You can experiment with one, two, or three yardsticks, extending them straight up in a gradual climb, end to end. You can build as many ramps as you want, end to end.

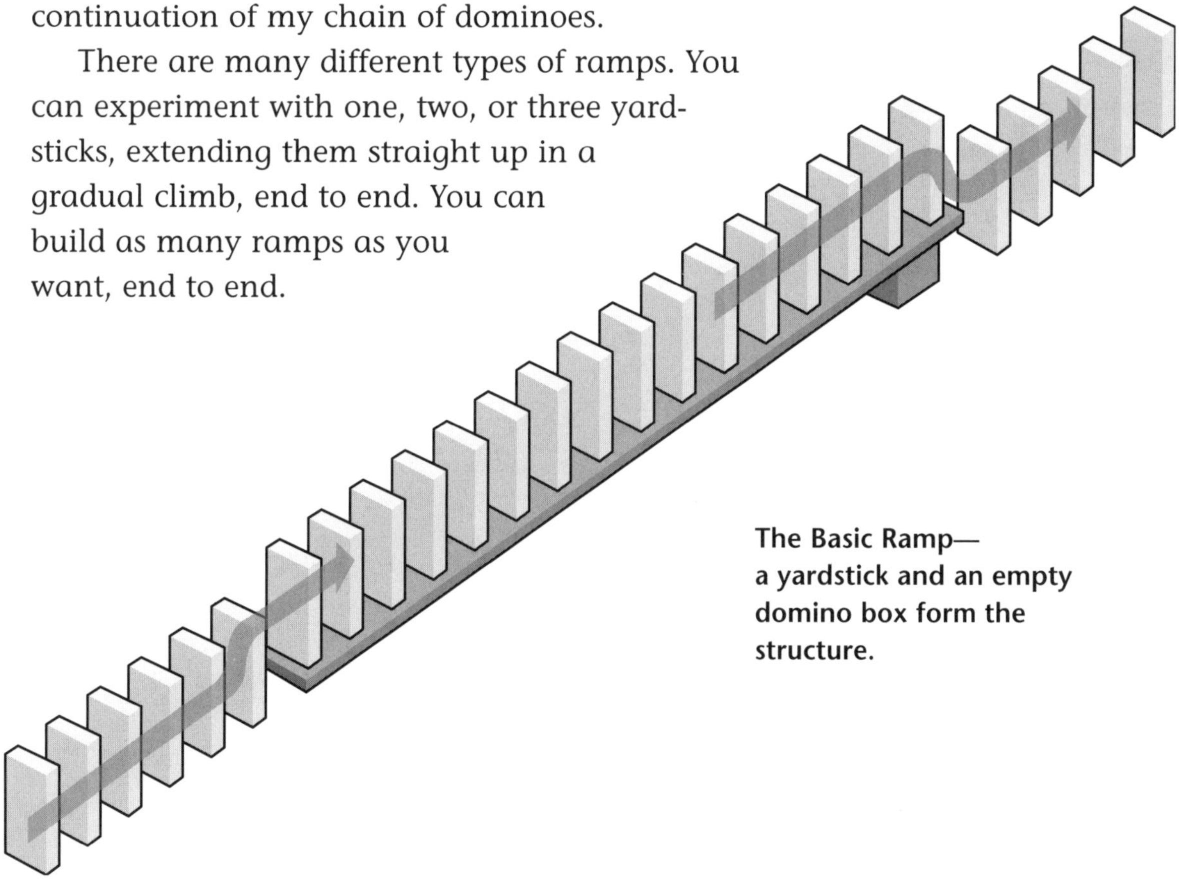

**The Basic Ramp—
a yardstick and an empty
domino box form the
structure.**

I've built 17 ramps to get up as high as a pool table. The trick is to keep increasing the number of boxes underneath (one to two boxes under the first yardstick, two to three under the next yardstick, and so on). For variation, you can try T-ramps, made by placing another yardstick at the top of the elevated yardstick (supported by domino boxes on both sides). The domino lines will run perpendicular to each other, with the two ends stopping dead or the dominoes dropping off to start another chain.

One variation of the Ramp, which I used on *The Tonight Show*, is called Dueling Ramps, a takeoff on "Dueling Banjos." Carson, as do most people who see it, responded by saying, "Here they come...get a load of the Dueling Ramps." By strict

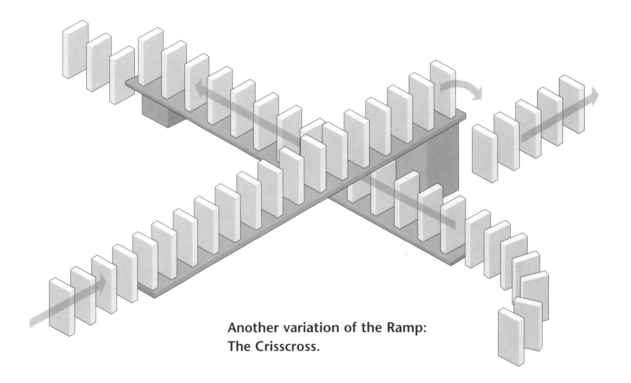

**Another variation of the Ramp: The Crisscross.**

definition, Dueling Ramps consists of just two ramps, but you
can have as many as you want.
It's just a matter of having a
split-off before each ramp, right
up to the first domino at the
bottom of the yardstick.

The two ramps in Dueling
Ramps topple at the same time,
but in opposite directions.
Although they are parallel to
each other—about two inches
apart—one rises from left to

**Dueling Ramps.**

right and the other from right to left. You start with a split-off
at the foot of each yardstick—one split-off going to the right
and the other to the left. Both split-offs simultaneously trigger
the first domino up the ramps. From floor level it looks as if
they are passing each other right where the intersection is—
say, at about 18 inches on the yardstick—going in opposite
directions at the same time.

As an added effect, instead of having the last domino hit
another on the floor to continue the chain, you can make it fall
into a glass of water, a box, or just about anything else you can
think of. I've had the dominoes fall off two separate ramps and
join again in a merge. In fact, *The Guinness Book of World Records*
credits me with having "dominoes split off and topple simultaneously along two ramps forming a letter V."

Patience is the better part of virtue with the Ramp. It will
reward you handsomely in the long run, if you are mentally
prepared for a long run.

# Ram's Horns

THE Ram's Horns are an extension of turns and split-offs. A spiral or pinwheel effect is created that looks very much like the design on the side of the St. Louis Rams' helmets.

In the show I put on in New York for the National Hemophilia Foundation, I built four with a diameter of two feet each, two of the spirals going clockwise and two counter-clockwise. The effect was mesmerizing.

The design is relatively simple to build: Coming up from the introductory trunk, construct two split-offs, one going right, the other left. Now, slowly build concentric turns that gradually spiral inward—sort of wheels within wheels, one going clockwise (the right side) and the other counterclockwise (the

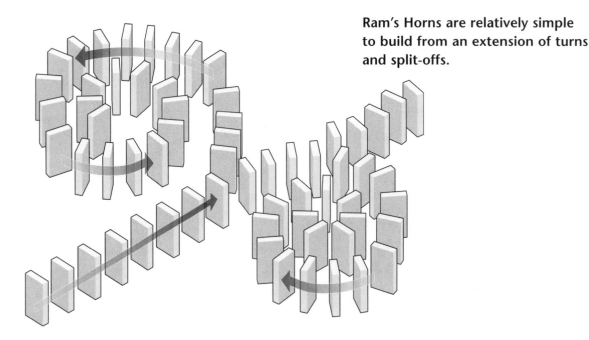

**Ram's Horns are relatively simple to build from an extension of turns and split-offs.**

left side). Those two spirals make up the Ram's Horns; the last domino inside the concentric circles dies out, and the chain carried on by the original trunk goes beyond the two split-offs.

Because the Ram's Horns are spirals from the outside *in*, you don't have to worry about how close you place the dominoes to one another. The outside dominoes will already have fallen by the time the inside ones fall; thus, there is virtually no chance of a mishap. (However, when a spiral goes from the inside *out*, leave room between the lines of dominoes, since momentum will cause the dominoes to fall outward and they will often hit the next row.)

Like most designs, the Ram's Horns have several variations. One of these is named for a friend of mine who suggested that if I could do two spirals, why not four? I did, and *voilà*, the Neivert Effect, which is really two Ram's Horns, with the split-off going completely around the design, encircling it in a fan-shaped rim.

**A sophisticated version of Ram's Horns: The Neivert Effect.**

One last note: You can heighten the effect of both the Ram's Horns and the Neivert Effect by using different-colored dominoes. Spray-paint them in rainbow colors to make the result look like a pinwheel going off.

**The Rams Horns and Integration (see page 55).**

# Triple and Super Peel-Offs

ONCE you've successfully built the Ram's Horns and the Neivert Effect, you can see how the splitting off of one line into two spirals (the Ram's Horns) and two into four (the Neivert Effect) can lead to any number of lines.

The next logical design, the Triple Peel-Off, is one of those extensions. In this design, the dominoes fall in a straight line; when one splits off into two lines, one of those lines goes straight and the other spirals off and continues around in a circle until it hits the original line—which has already fallen behind it. Then the straight line does it again, and still one more time, with spirals splitting off. Each of the spirals finishes in a dead end.

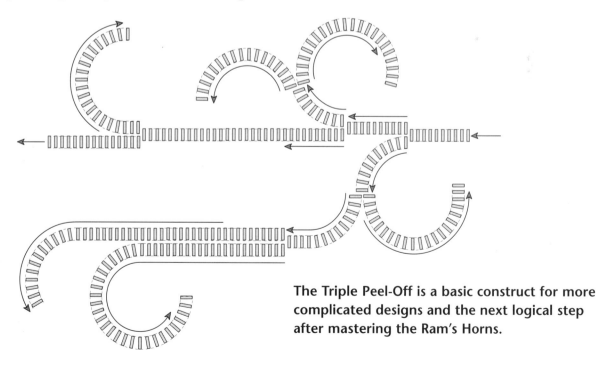

**The Triple Peel-Off is a basic construct for more complicated designs and the next logical step after mastering the Ram's Horns.**

Coming out of the Triple Peel-Off is still another design, one I call the Super Peel-Off. Imagine as many split-offs and spirals as possible from each side, then from each split-off another split-off and still another and another, like a grapevine, and you have the Super Peel-Off.

The effect is much like the old Tom and Jerry cartoon sequence in which hundreds of mouse-traps on the floor are triggered at once when Jerry throws a ping-pong ball in the middle. The Super Peel-Off works the same way. Before you know it, you have as many as 60 different rows falling, each growing out of another.

The Super Peel-Off is restricted only by the number of dominoes you want to use, with each spiral coming out of the basic trunk line and splitting off into what looks like an O—although it need not be complete and, in fact, could approximate a square, triangle, squiggly line, or anything you might want to use to differentiate it from a straight line. The tighter the spirals are, the more they look like fireworks going off one after another.

The Super Peel-Off is almost a guaranteed success. And because it is such a radical departure from straight lines, it creates more interest among audiences, and begets more than the usual oohs and aahs.

**A surefire showstopper: The Super Peel-Off.**

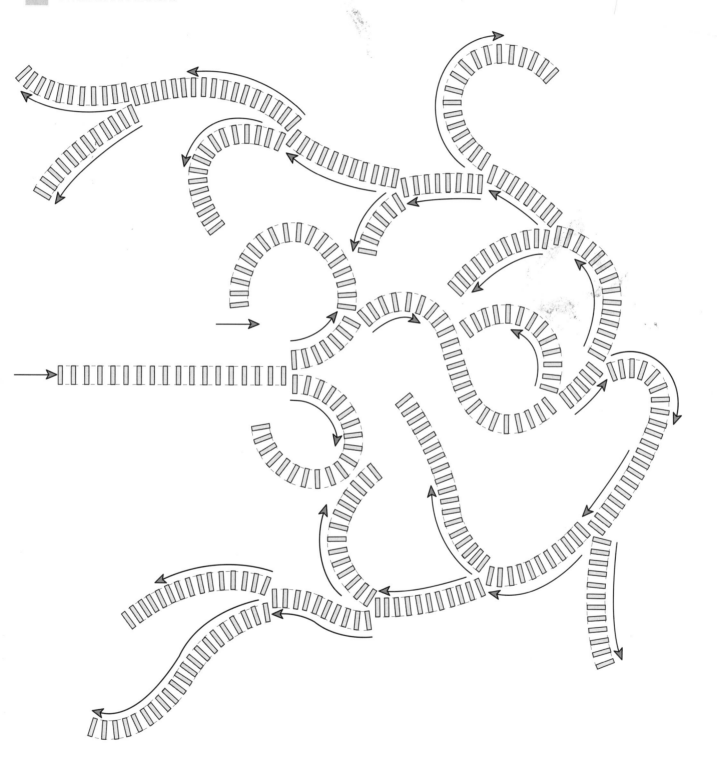

# Arachnid

◧◨ BY now, you should be bored with spirals. I know I was. That's why I came up with a design called Arachnid, the Greek word for spider, and characteristic of any arthropods in that class having four pairs of legs.

But it wasn't a love of Greek or of arthropods that inspired this creation. It was my favorite superhero, Spiderman. The spider (arachnid) was his trademark, so I concocted this design as a tribute to him. (Your experimentation and imagination could lead you to develop designs for your own superheroes, whether they are Wonder Woman, Batman, the Hulk, the Daredevil, or someone else from your childhood.)

Because a spider has four pairs of legs, the Arachnid has eight legs—and eight split-offs. The tentacles can be as long as you want. I have made them almost a yard long in some of my setups, trying to make them look like a spider's so they can be easily identified.

A word of caution: The Arachnid has many intersections with a Triple Split-off (one going straight, one going to the left, and one to the right), and the traffic jam it creates in a small area is not unlike that in the letters X and K, which makes it difficult to set up.

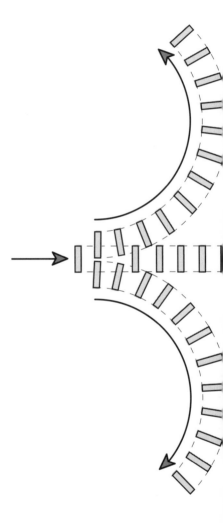

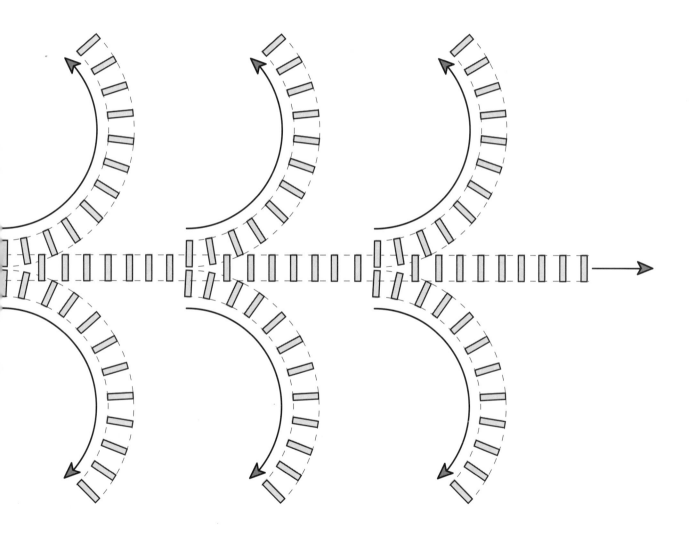

**Arachnid is a tribute to Spiderman constructed of eight split-offs.**

# Delayed Dynamic Dozen

THE Delayed Dynamic Dozen is just what the name implies: a *dozen* rows make up the design; it is *delayed*, because none of the domino lines falls at the same time; and it is *dynamic*, because it's an energetic design, providing an exciting effect.

The design is a simple extension of the split-off and the Super Peel-Off, but instead of peeling off, the split-offs topple in straight lines—twelve of them, to be exact, looking like a Hanukkah menorah with three extra branches.

The basic concept for the Delayed Dynamic Dozen is generating split-offs from split-offs. There is one split-off from the baseline coming up into the design, and then from each of the two limbs there are six more split-offs, for a total of twelve branches, in a perfectly symmetrical form.

Each of the branches goes straight up (rather than spiraling) and, as it goes off, dies out at the end, with the chain continued on by either of the main limbs.

**In the Delayed Dynamic Dozen, split-offs and Super Peel-Offs combine in a fireworks effect.**

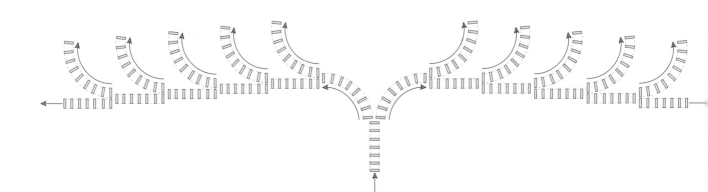

# The Eight Rows, or Integration

■□ IF one domino can split off and hit two dominoes, forming two lines, it stands to reason that from those two you can make two more straight lines, and two branching off into four. Or four into eight. Or any other number you want, ad infinitum.

One trick that always elicits a great number of "oohs" and "aahs" from those watching is the toppling of eight rows at once—which is nothing more than split-offs from split-offs from an initial split-off. That's the basic idea behind split-offs, to have them flow into a lot of other designs.

The Eight Rows is a lot like the Delayed Dynamic Dozen, except that it's more complicated in design and takes a little longer to set up.

As in the Delayed Dynamic Dozen, one introductory, or trunk, line comes into the design and immediately splits off into two lines. The two lines go in opposite directions, approximately 18 inches around the outside of the design, making the formation about a yard in circumference. These two lines then hook around and each splits off twice, with each of those split-offs splitting off still another time—sort of a double split-off, with the left line dead-ending in the eighth row and the right line going on to continue the chain.

The lines formed within the boundaries of the two original lines are approximately thirty-six inches long, and are parallel to each other to give the effect of the claws of a crab.

In the Eight Rows, rows 2, 4, 6, and 8 go from left to right, and rows 1, 3, 5, and 7 from right to left. The effect is that of two sets of fingers intertwined. To heighten the visual effect, you can use two sets of different-colored dominoes, painting one set of rows white and leaving the other (say the 1, 3, 5, and 7 rows) black. This two-color design, which I call Integration, produces one of the most pleasurable visual effects of any design I incorporate in my setup, no matter how advanced. (The dominoes can also be alternately colored red and blue.) It usually takes about 20 minutes to set up for one second of fun. But it's worth it!

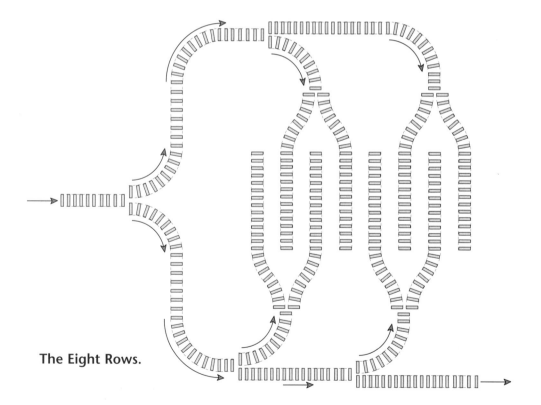

**The Eight Rows.**

From Eight Rows, it's a simple matter to go on to the next trick: four split-offs forming the American flag, 13 rows in all, all falling at the same time and in the same direction—from left to right. In this trick, 12 of the parallel lines dead-end and the 13th, the bottom line, goes on to the next design.

It takes 30 minutes to set up and only a second and a half for all 13 rows to fall over. The effect, however, is stunning, especially if you spray-paint the dominoes red, white, and blue and put in a small wrinkle (or turn) to make the flag look as if it's waving. But be careful not to place the lines too close together so that they hit each other.

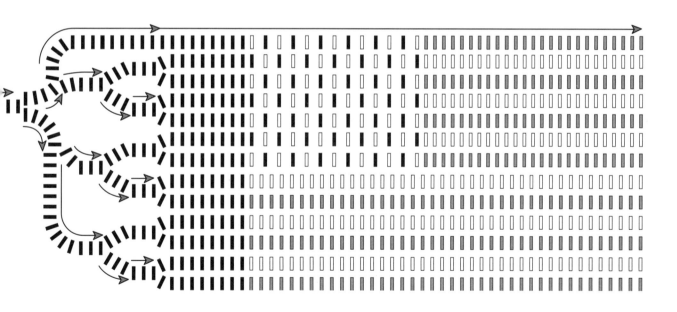

**A stunning effect in color:
The American flag.**

# The Diamond

ROY Campanella once said, "You have to have a lot of little boy in you to play baseball for a living." I guess that holds true for domino-toppling, too. And sometimes it even affects my designs.

Take, for instance, the Diamond, which is really a backward-and-forward split-off. I've always been a fan of Neil Diamond, even to the point of having him sign a playing card for me—the ace of diamonds, naturally. In his honor, I designed the Diamond.

Most of my designs are constructed to fall in one direction. The Diamond is one of the few designs I have that works both backward and forward. You can set it up either way. As such, you can place it anywhere you want in your total design and hit it coming from either side.

You don't need a split-off with the Diamond because it is in itself a split-off, which, when finished, becomes its own continuation, exiting out the bottom and going on to the next design.

The Diamond is easy to construct, requiring only that you set up all the dominoes so they face the same way. As you set them up, move each succeeding domino about one-third of the way off the outside shoulder of the previous one, so they look like soldiers moving out in a diagonal formation. Thus, with each domino taking only two-thirds the space of the one before it, the sides of the design are extended, while at the same time the striking domino is provided with enough surface area to hit.

After you have lined up approximately 20 dominoes in this staggered formation, begin to bring them back toward the middle, reverse the procedure, and place them one-third of the way off the inside shoulder. Repeat on the other side for the four sides of the diamond and connect the dominoes to a trunk line exiting out of the Diamond in order to carry on the chain.

You'll find that the Diamond is a novel way of setting up dominoes, and also a novel way of forming a split-off.

By combining the Diamond with the Ramp, you can adapt the design to make an Elevated Square or Box Ramp, similar in shape to a baseball diamond. In this design, the ramps are elevated so that the ends go up on the sides (first and third base) and continue up, toward where second base would be. Unlike the Diamond, this is not a split-off that continues; it dies off at the top.

**The Diamond is a backward-and-forward split-off designed in honor of Neil Diamond.**

# Intersections: The Figure Eight

■□■ **I**NTERSECTIONS are among the most difficult maneuvers. Yet they are instrumental in building complicated designs, especially Advanced ones.

The most elementary intersection is a figure eight, a configuration made by a line of dominoes that goes through a standing line and comes back to cross over what has already fallen, thus creating a loop.

Intersections are almost always perpendicular, which means that the line that comes back across the already fallen dominoes should be at right angles to the line of dominoes that has fallen. Otherwise, the dominoes might not surmount those that have fallen in the first part of the crossover.

One way to ensure success is to use two different sizes of dominoes. What? You thought dominoes came in only one size? Not so. As mentioned earlier, dominoes come in various sizes besides the standard one-and-a-half inch. There are one-and-three-quarter-inch dominoes and larger and smaller ones sold in specialty stores.

After much experimentation, I found that by using smaller-sized dominoes on the line that falls across the intersection first, and larger ones on the line that loops back and crosses over to create the intersection, I had a much greater chance of success—almost 100 percent, as opposed to just over 60 percent with same-size dominoes. When I used same-size dominoes for both lines, the first line often fell and clogged the intended intersection.

It must be remembered that success in engineering an intersection depends on getting as much as possible of the striking surface of the domino located in the crossover line to hit the domino on the other side as it moves over the fallen dominoes. If the fallen dominoes are the same size as the striking domino and the one being hit, they often prevent the all-important strike. Smaller dominoes on the first line usually leave a gap for the crossover line, and make for a successful figure eight.

The intersection might not work the first few times you try it. But with a little practice, it *will* work, especially if you use smaller dominoes and leave enough room so that the first line can go through and the striking domino on the line that comes back over can hit the domino on the other side, triggering the line going out of the figure eight.

**With the figure eight, the secret to success is using two different sizes of dominoes.**

# Triple Intersections and DNA

STILL another type of intersection is the Triple Intersection. If you can do one intersection, as in the figure eight, you can do three just as easily. What the Triple Intersection is all about is a spiral from the *inside out*, instead of the outside in, as we used in the Ram's Horns.

To form the Triple Intersection, or the spiral from the inside out, start with a line that falls straight. When it gets to a certain point, give it a very sharp turn and have it come back on itself, just like a regular intersection. Have the line cross over the pieces that have already fallen and keep spiraling outward, much like a reverse Ram's Horns (only a reverse Ram's Horns won't work unless you can do the intersection). The line comes around—looking in some respects like an overgrown marigold, or any other shape you want (square, triangular, or even squiggly)—and intersects three times.

Always, *always*, do a split-off before you go into your intersection, to ensure that any foul-up won't end your entire design. A foul-up has happened to me more than once, even on national television!

Once you've mastered the figure eight and the Triple Intersection, you can experiment with more advanced intersections, such as the DNA. The DNA (which stands for deoxyribonucleic acid), or Double Helix, is two lines joined together,

crossing over and over again in a tightly woven chain. Don't let the name throw you. It's almost longer than the trick. All this design consists of, is two figure Eight's—or as many as you want— which require different-sized dominoes.

An elaborate domino-toppling setup that features the DNA (at top of photo) and the Tarzan Swing (on the far left), which is discussed on page 77.
*Photo courtesy of Mark Monroe.*

When I was on *The Tonight Show*, Johnny Carson asked me, "What do you call that again?" And I rattled off the name a second time. Carson looked at the camera and said, "That's why we call it DNA, because no one can say the whole name." You'll find that before you can pronounce the name of the trick, you'll be able to do it.

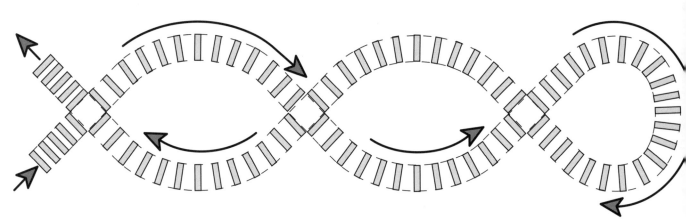

**The DNA: The full name is longer than the trick and not nearly as much fun.**

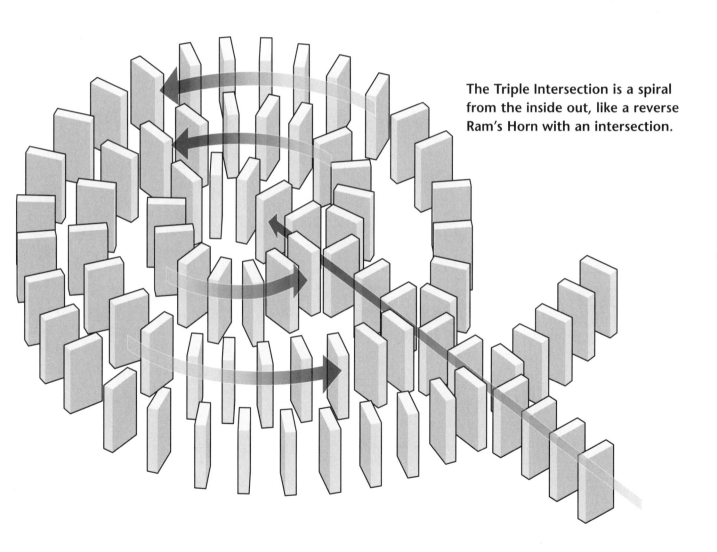

The Triple Intersection is a spiral from the inside out, like a reverse Ram's Horn with an intersection.

# ADVANCED DESIGNS

# The Edge Ramp

■■ WE now move into what I call the Advanced Designs. By the time you've reached this level, you should be able to make elaborate displays out of dominoes.

For the first time—with the notable exception of the Ramp, which used a yardstick—you will include other items besides dominoes in your designs. The first of these designs is the Edge Ramp, a direct descendant of the Ramp. For this we will use a meterstick instead of a yardstick.

A meterstick, as you undoubtedly know, measures a meter instead of a yard; meters are the fundamental measure of length in the metric system (there are 39.37 inches in a meter, in contrast to the 36 inches in a yard). It also differs from a yardstick in that it is thicker—the equivalent of two yardsticks taped together. Turned on its side, it will balance without any props to steady it.

Standing the meterstick, or ramp, on its edge, set the dominoes up along the edge of the ramp so that half of each domino is actually hanging over the edge of the ramp, centered perfectly. Granted, this requires a steady hand, but with patience and practice, you'll be able to do it.

When all the dominoes are centered in the middle, you should see an interesting and arresting effect: The dominoes, with the exception of the last one, will usually stay on the ramp even after they've fallen. The last one will fall off and continue the design, or, in the case of a split-off, finish in a dead end.

There are variations on this basic theme. You can place all the dominoes on one edge of the ramp so that they will all fall to one side. Or you can alternate them, one to each side. And, of course, the Edge Ramp, lying flat, will work from either direction.

Another variation on the basic Edge Ramp is achieved by elevating the ramp with a domino box to form a runway. While this can only be approached from one direction, you will find that if the elevation isn't too severe, the dominoes will still fall on the meterstick.

The primary requirement for executing the Edge Ramp successfully is patience. Setting up the dominoes on the edge of the meterstick will take many, many attempts to do correctly.

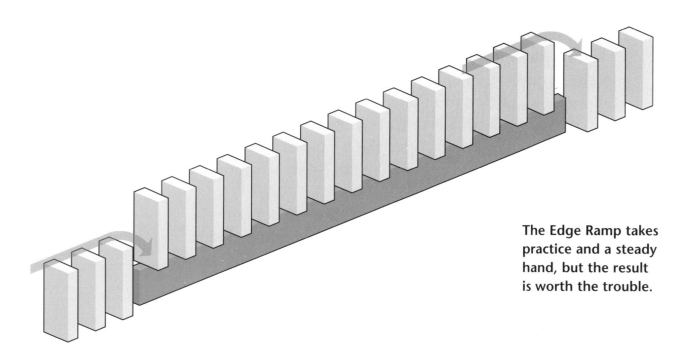

**The Edge Ramp takes practice and a steady hand, but the result is worth the trouble.**

# The Balloon

■■ THE Balloon is my "closer"—something I save for the end of my act—but because we're progressing from easiest to hardest in this book, it should be learned before you go on to the hand-built contraptions.

To accomplish the Balloon requires merely the ability to blow up a balloon, tie it, and securely place it where, as the finale to your act, it can be burst.

Have the balloon go off at the end of your act because the pieces of popped balloon will act like shrapnel, flying all over the room, and at any other point in your act they could set off another part of your design. The mere force of air escaping from the balloon could blow over some of your dominoes.

For the Balloon, you need a domino with a hole in the top containing a rod with a pin in it that punctures the balloon. This can be made by almost anyone. A friend of mine, notoriously unhandy and unable to fix anything, constructed one by wrapping some tape at the top of the domino after making a hole and inserting a rod holding the pin, with the sharp part extended above the domino.

That's not all there is to it, however. The balloon must be blown up pretty tightly, almost to the point of self-explosion. Otherwise, when the pin hits it, it will not break it, but merely nudge it, which is not what you want for your ending. Also, the balloon must be taped to the floor to secure it for the falling domino pin and to prevent it from wafting away with the first rush of air. Finally, the little rod holding the pin must be high enough to ensure that the falling domino has enough velocity to puncture the balloon when striking it at the proper perpendicular angle. And it must contain a sharp pin, of course.

Sometimes, no matter how well you've prepared your ending, there's a foul-up. The balloon goes off prematurely because it's been blown up too tightly or the pin isn't sharp enough to puncture it. So, although this trick sounds easy, if you're planning to use it as a boffo ending, you must make sure everything is carefully prepared. Then stand back!

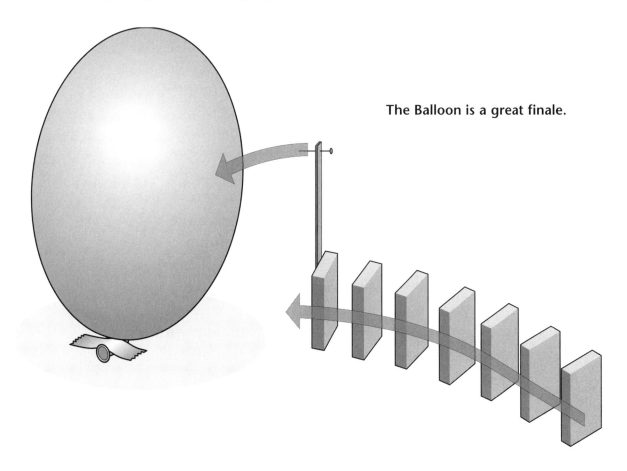

**The Balloon is a great finale.**

# The Mousetrap

THE other ending I often use is the Mousetrap. It's done with plain old ordinary mousetraps sold at the hardware store. I was playing with some mousetraps—and considering using them in my act—when some kids suggested I try shooting them across the room and hitting another domino 20 feet away. Well, I started fooling around, catching my finger in the traps more times than I care to admit, and found that although I couldn't control the trajectory of the trap to the point where it could hit something across a room with any degree of accuracy, an activated mousetrap would make one heck of a finale.

The key words here are *be careful*, not only of your fingers (I still get my finger caught in the bar about once in every 20 times I set one up), but also of the dominoes in your display. If you use the Mousetrap anywhere but at the end of your design, you're asking for trouble, because the domino resting on the bar will likely fly back into some standing dominoes and start a chain reaction you hadn't planned on. You have to be careful even when you use it at the end of your design because when you're setting it up, it can go off prematurely and ruin two to three hours of painstaking work.

Setting up the Mousetrap is simple enough, particularly if you have patience and dexterous fingers. Using a standard mousetrap, you can approach it with an introductory line and place a domino on the bent end of the bar that snaps to catch the mouse. Don't place it directly on top of the bar, but a litte

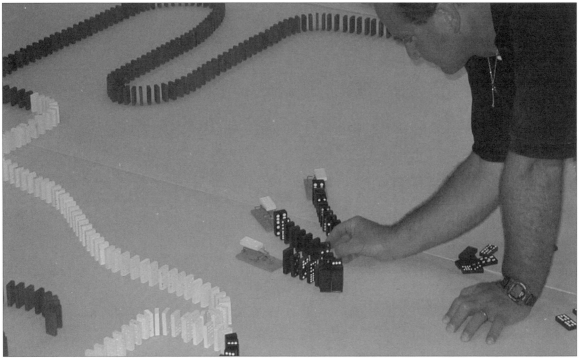

*Photo courtesy of Mark Monroe.*

**Setting up the Mousetrap.**

behind it. That way, when the trap is jostled and the spring snaps, the domino will fly up in the air—but not until then (you hope). To prevent it from going off prematurely, face the trap toward the audience, or away from your design. That way, if a mishap occurs, the domino will fly *away* from the standing dominoes, not into them. But don't put the trap too close to another portion of your design, because if it goes off prematurely, the recoil of the spring will jar the trap back into the standing dominoes.

Another reason the Mousetrap is used at the end and not during the act is that although you know the general direction in which the domino on the bar will fly, you have no idea *exactly* where it will go. It's impossible to hit something on the

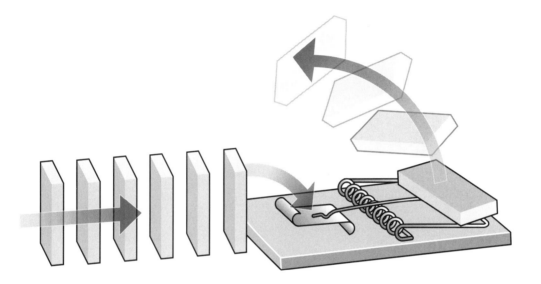

floor to continue the chain because the reaction is too helter-skelter.

If you want a really big ending, have a whole bunch of mousetraps go off. This is done through a series of split-offs leading up to the numerous mousetraps. You can try many other effects, including having two traps snap at the same time and meet in midair (I must warn you, this is not as easy as it sounds). You can also alternate traps, so that they go off in all four directions, or crisscross. But whatever you do, do it at the end.

**The Mousetrap is set up facing away from your main design so a mishap won't ruin the rest of your design.**

# The High Dive

⬛⬛ WE now move into the world of wooden contraptions. Some of them are built to look like Rube Goldberg contrivances; others are exactly what they look like—home-built, simpler devices. And most of them are not only the suggestions of friends, but were built by them as well.

The first one in this category is the High Dive (also known as the Vertical Ramp, or Slow-Motion Escalator), built by a high-school buddy, Larry Kushner. Looking for all the world like an escalator that has stopped, it has 28 little notches, set up about one inch apart and angled at about 45 degrees, so that the steps are horizontal to the surface. The base is made of wood and anchored to the ramp. For more stability, I tape the entire contraption to the floor.

Because this contraption is, at best, precarious, I set it up at the beginning of the act and work around it. Otherwise, the dominoes that fall off the ramp could trigger some of the other lines in my design.

The principle underlying the High Dive is that the dominoes must stand up straight in order to fall over. The angle at which the dominoes are positioned allows them to move in slow motion up the ramp at about 4 or 5 per second (instead of the 35 to 40 you get in a regular line on the floor). It also allows you to get to a higher height a lot faster than the ramps we've built before. In fact, it's about the same height as 12 metersticks placed end to end.

The reason the dominoes fall at a slower rate of speed is

that they don't have as much of a surface to hit because they are striking the next domino at a much lower level than normal, somewhere around the base.

I call this trick the High Dive because the last domino, poised on the top, looks much like an Acapulco cliff diver. Not only does the domino look like a cliff diver, it performs like one, doing a one-and-a-half somersault with a full twist into a glass of water.

Obviously, there is a split-off before the High Dive because there is no guarantee that anything somersaulting from a height of 18 inches will hit anything on the floor. It has been done. But I would never plan my entire design around it—too chancy.

**In the High Dive, the angle allows the dominoes to fall in slow motion up the ramp.**

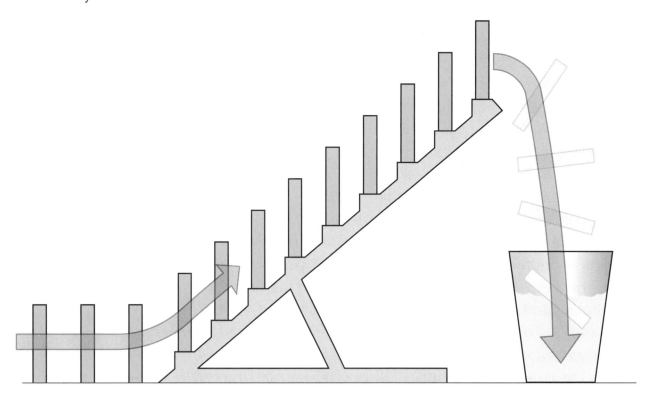

# Kushner's Tarzan Swing

⬛⬛ THE second of my seven wooden contraptions has a Rube Goldberg look, with dominoes triggering dominoes, which cause others to fall, et cetera. The only thing missing here is a cat chasing a mouse to power the machine.

Built by, and named for, Larry Kushner, this device, coming after a split-off, allows one domino to swing from the top of a vertical ramp, such as the one we just built, across what most writers would call a yawning chasm to a platform on the other side, where it hits another row of dominoes.

The ramp (or diving board, in this case) has but 16 steps and is only half as long as the High Dive. The last domino at the top of the ramp is secured by two pieces of string or dental

**The Tarzan Swing.**

floss to a pair of hooks attached to a vertical "gallows" about ten inches away. The two hooks allow the domino attached to it to swing freely. One hook might not allow it to swing in a straight line, which is necessary if the swinging domino is to hit the line on the platform on the other side.

Flying through the air with the greatest of ease, and accuracy, the Tarzan-like domino spans 14 inches and strikes the domino on the other side. This striking action was something that Larry figured out only after a lot of false starts and practice.

The last domino on the platform across the way can fall into a glass of water or be attached to something else, like a ramp going down, a balloon, or the Elevator (described on pages 84 to 86).

The intricate mechanics are worth it! This trick seems to be everybody's favorite. And you can ham it up by putting a loincloth on the swinging domino, or foliage underneath, or by screaming "AAAAAAAH" as the domino swings over.

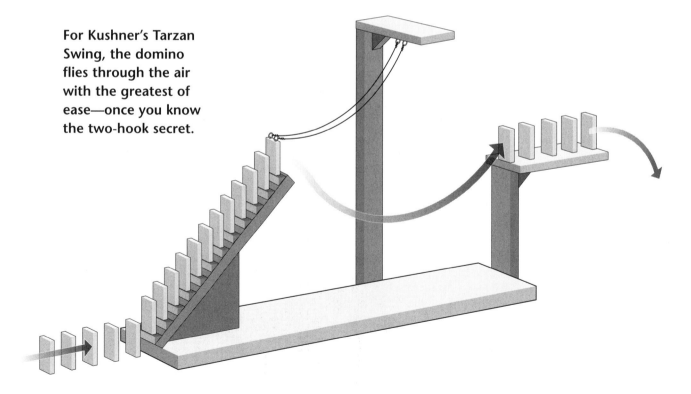

For Kushner's Tarzan Swing, the domino flies through the air with the greatest of ease—once you know the two-hook secret.

# Bahama Tom Inverted Cascade Slide for Life

**◼◼** A S the contraptions get more complicated, so do the names. This one—the Bahama Tom Inverted Cascade Slide for Life—was named after the guy who thought up the idea and the plans for it. (Tom wasn't from the Bahamas, but he had vacationed there and we called him Bahama Tom.)

The Bahama Tom Inverted Cascade Slide for Life is the quickest method of getting dominoes to a higher altitude besides just throwing them into the air. It's done without ramps and without steps—but with a lot of ingenuity.

The Bahama Tom Inverted Cascade Slide for Life.

In order to get the dominoes off the floor so I would have more variety in my act, I had experimented with building as many as 17 ramps to get up to the height of a pool table. But the Bahama Tom got me to that height in two seconds, and with a lot less dominoes—approximately 50.

It works on almost the same principle as the Tarzan Swing (much as graduating from the Ramp to the Edge Ramp is an extension of the same principle). However, the Bahama Tom has one other aspect to it—four platforms instead of just one.

Here the four platforms are formed by four horizontal pieces of wood, creating an effect that looks like something out of a Roadrunner cartoon. And it performs essentially the same function as the devices the coyote builds to propel an anvil or rock into the air. Each of the platforms has a dowel at the end, placed through a Tinkertoy spool that, when hit, pivots 90 degrees and continues the chain by hitting the dominoes on the next higher level.

This process is repeated three times until the last domino at the end of the top platform is hit, causing that domino— which I call Geronimo Domino—to slide down a long thin wire (which is attached to a gallows and is almost invisible) and strike another on a platform a full two feet away.

A platform rests on a wood base block of about nine to ten inches. This base block supports two other blocks of wood, which, in turn, support three platforms, giving the contraption the appearance of a large H. The platforms create an exciting illusion of dominoes falling in a staccato fashion with a slight pause, while the dowels,

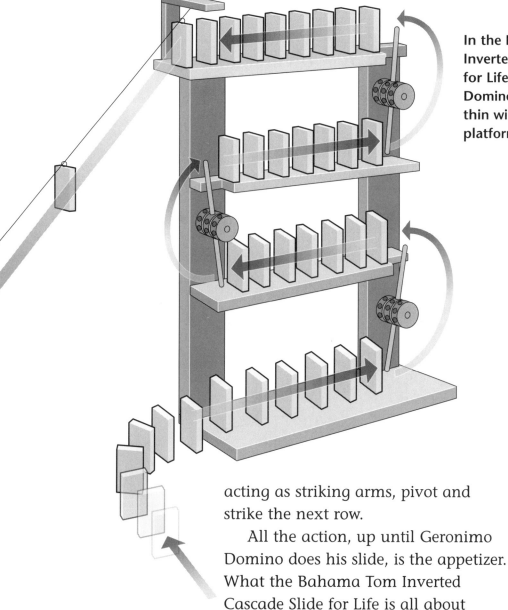

**In the Bahama Tom Inverted Cascade Slide for Life, Geronimo Domino slides down a thin wire, aided by platforms and Tinkertoys.**

acting as striking arms, pivot and strike the next row.

All the action, up until Geronimo Domino does his slide, is the appetizer. What the Bahama Tom Inverted Cascade Slide for Life is all about is the slide.

I usually link the Bahama Tom with another of my wooden contraptions, most often the Tarzan Swing, to heighten the effect of the dominoes simultaneously falling on the floor.

# Walking the Plank

WALKING the Plank is exactly what it sounds like, and is an extension of the Bahama Tom.

This trick requires that a domino fall onto a launching pad, usually from a wooden contraption that has given the domino the right height and trajectory, causing a dowel in a Tinkertoy spool to pivot and hit yet another dowel. This, in turn, knocks over the six or so dominoes on a high platform, the last one of which then does a one-and-a-half gainer onto the floor. Or into a water glass.

Obviously, the chances of the last domino hitting some other domino on the floor with any degree of accuracy are slight, at best. Therefore, Walking the Plank—and the other tricks in this section—comes off a split-off, the other part of which is doing something that is more assured of success. This way, whatever happens cannot ruin the entire effect, only heighten it.

**Walking the Plank.**

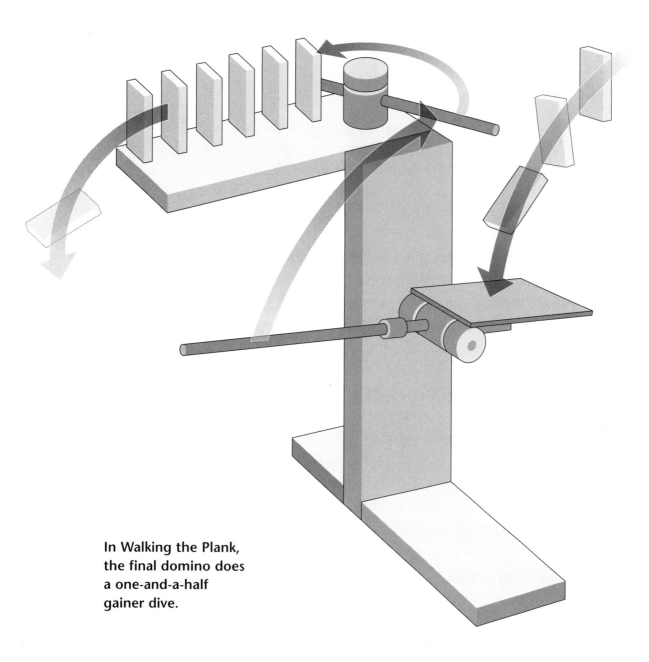

In Walking the Plank,
the final domino does
a one-and-a-half
gainer dive.

# The Elevator

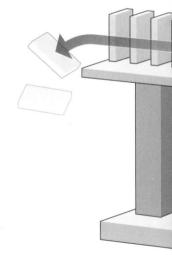

THE Elevator is the one moment in the show when *no* dominoes are falling. Not only is the Elevator a radical departure from the normal progression of domino knocking over domino, but the pause it provides grabs the audience's attention—both visually and audibly.

The Elevator is merely two pieces of wood with two pulleys attached that rotate a long piece of fishing wire. The wire alternately pulls a little basket at one end of the contrivance and a little elevator platform at the other. When one goes up, the other goes down, like a scale.

It is this delicate balance that controls the operation of the mechanism—and the trick. When the elevator platform is filled with four dominoes, it must await the movement of the little platform across the way to start ascending. It is that ascension, *and* a strategically placed nail that hits the first of the four dominoes in the elevator when it gets up to a certain level, that knocks over the six dominoes on the way station adjacent to the elevator and continues the chain.

In order to create the delayed reaction and operate the Elevator, a way must be found to get up to the height of the first platform that faces the open basket. I usually use something like the Bahama Tom, the Tarzan Swing, or a 45-degree ramp. In the illustration here, I have used the 45-degree Elevated Ramp to get up to the platform, with the previous domino from the end of the 45-degree ramp striking the five or six dominoes that are waiting there facing the pulley, much

like passengers waiting to enter an elevator. Only these domino passengers are awaiting a basket.

As the line of dominoes falls, one or two fall into the basket. The weight of those dominoes is enough to counter the
weight of the four on the elevator, causing it to rise in inverse
proportion to the falling basket. When the elevator rises to the
proper height (which is exactly the same height as the second

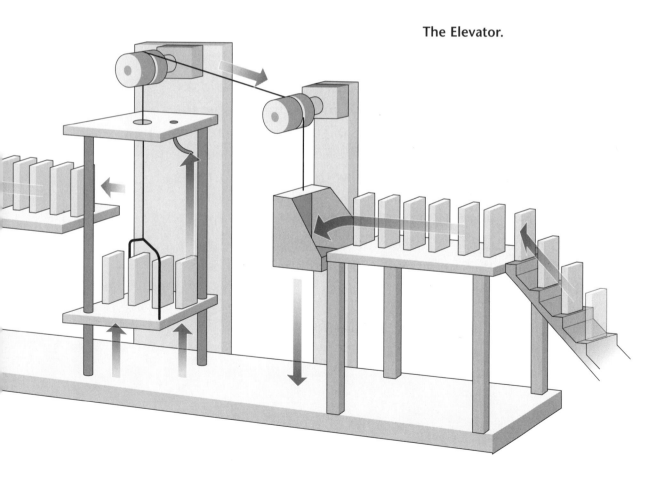

**The Elevator.**

platform or way station) so that those six dominoes and the four in the elevator are one continuous line of ten, the back domino in the elevator is hit by a nail embedded in the top, and the chain starts.

The last domino on the platform can fall into a glass of water or whatever. Maybe you've already used up all the glasses in your house and have to think of some other receptacle for dominoes to topple into.

Though the Elevator sounds confusing, it is relatively simple and works according to a scientific principle, namely, that for every action there is an equal and opposite reaction. That, and a nail, account for what might well be one of your most unusual tricks.

The Elevator lends itself to several other designs. One looks like a production number from a 1930s movie. In this one, the 45-degree ramp splits off into four sets of stairs going across a horizontal plane and onto the platform. The pulley system is retained, except that a wide-neck cup, with a bottom narrower than the top, is attached to the other end instead of an elevator. The cup acts much like the elevator, but instead of hitting a nail and triggering the four dominoes standing inside it, the domino falls from the cup onto a starburst pattern and detonates it.

# Six Days Till Sunday

■■ SIX Days Till Sunday, so named because six elevated platforms come off a base, is the most spectacular of all elevated designs, rivaling the most spectacular floor design, the American flag.

Although it looks well nigh impossible to construct, the mechanism is simply six platforms, each shorter than the one below; a pulley made up of a domino hooked onto a wire; a fishing weight that acts as a pulley to provide the proper rate of ascension for the hooked domino; and a dowel and Tinkertoy spool upon which another domino is secured by a hook.

To set up Six Days Till Sunday—Sunday being the top platform—first place a domino on the very end of each platform, making sure it is poised like a diver on the high diving board. Then roll up the string on the Tinkertoy spool and bring the pulley up to the top of the gallows and the hooked domino down to the bottom. If you place all 250 of your dominoes in position first and then improperly wind up the fishing weight, you risk upsetting not only them, but also any nearby dominoes they may chance to hit.

Next, place the dominoes in position, starting with the activator (first domino) on each platform level. This way, you can see that they are properly lined up along the string so they can all be hit in the center. Then set up in the following sequence: the bottom row (Monday) first, then the second row (Tuesday), up to the top row (Sunday), thus ensuring that a top-heavy imbalance of dominoes will not cause the contraption to shake and knock over the dominoes prematurely.

Six Days Till Sunday starts off with an introductory line of dominoes knocking over the dominoes on the bottom platform, up to the dowel at the end. That triggers the hooked domino, which in turn activates the fishing weight. Ascending slowly as the pulley falls, the hooked domino begins to knock over the first domino on each platform, activating that row. By the time the hooked domino gets to the next level, the dominoes on the previous platform should be directly underneath the first, or activator, domino on the succeeding platform. Thus, when the hooked domino gets to the seventh level, all the dominoes on the preceding levels should

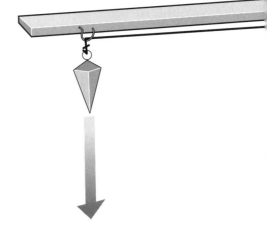

have fallen to the exact point where the seventh platform starts, with the still-standing dominoes lined up in perfect symmetry.

As each of the six rows going from left to right comes down its fallen file, the timing of Six Days Till Sunday calls for the domino at the end of each of the six elevated platforms to fall off at *exactly* the same time.

I've experimented with having all six fall into a waterwheel, which causes it to spin and start another contraption.

They can fall into a goldfish bowl or even a large glass vase. But they're not all going to make it into a glass. And they're obviously not going to be able to hit another design on the floor with any degree of accuracy.

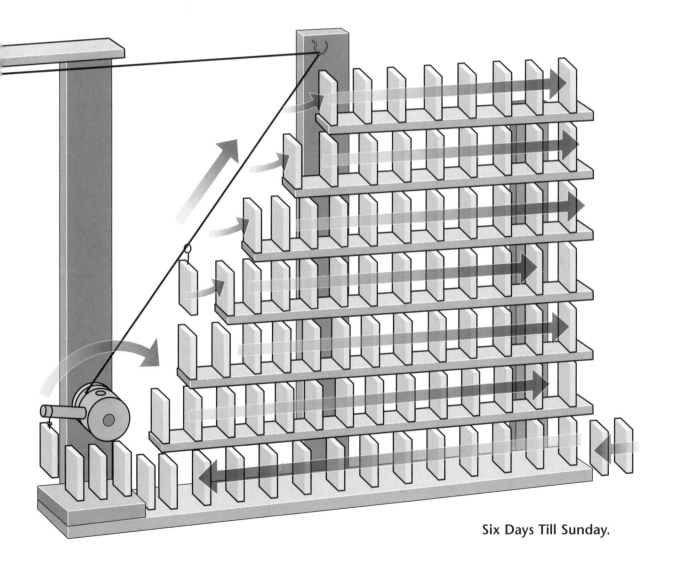

**Six Days Till Sunday.**

# Up the Mountain

THIS is the most cumbersome contraption I have to transport—a huge vertical spiral made up of columns, a six-foot wooden coil, and the imagination of a friend, who helped me construct it one night. In fact, the story behind Up the Mountain is almost as interesting as the effect it creates. I had long envisioned such an effect, but had never gotten around to creating it. Finally, when David Frost was putting together his *Guinness Book of World Records* program, his staff contacted me, knowing I had appeared twice on *The Tonight Show* and the Mike Douglas show and had undoubtedly exhausted my entire repertoire. As we discussed what I would do, I got the distinct impression they were trying to think of ways not to include me. Then I mentioned that I had a vertical spiral.

"Oh, a vertical spiral!" they said. "That sounds really impressive." Now I had my ticket to the ball. All I needed was a vertical whatever.

I had described it to the producers of the show as a road running around the outside of a mountain with the last domino falling through and hitting one on the ground, starting a new chain. But outside of a mental picture, I had no idea of how to build one. And I was scheduled to go on the show the following day.

Fortunately, I had a friend who was gifted in translating ideas into reality. Together we were able to convert six feet of coil made from one piece of wood (cut into a spiral with a jigsaw) into a mountainside in six hours—complete with columns and paint. Up the Mountain appeared for the first time on the David Frost Show, without the benefit of a tryout!

The contraption is just a piece of board, cut like an apple peel into one continuous spiral, and lifted up through the center and held in place by columns to create a birthday cake or beehive effect.

The vertical spiral is mathematically calibrated so that no matter what the spirals look like, the dominoes actually climb at the same rate and same angle as on a regular ramp the

**Up the Mountain.**

entire way up the mountain—at about nine degrees. They appear to be climbing at a faster rate at the top of the mountain because there is less distance in each concentric circle, but this is an illusion.

Now that we've explained the why and the what, let's look at *how* Up the Mountain works. Some 350 to 400 dominoes go round and round the spiral, much like a ramp, taking almost ten seconds to climb to the top, where the last one falls into the center. I vary it a little by creating a split-off at the very end and having two dominoes fall into the center, which gives me more of a chance of hitting the one on the ground and continuing the chain.

The height attained by Up the Mountain can be duplicated with step ramps done in a circular fashion. In this manner, the domino could fall from a height of about 12 inches. Or you might devise a collapsible contraption that wouldn't be as cumbersome to carry.

As a finale, you could have the top domino fall from the top of the structure wearing a little parachute, which would slow down its fall and keep it afloat for almost two seconds.

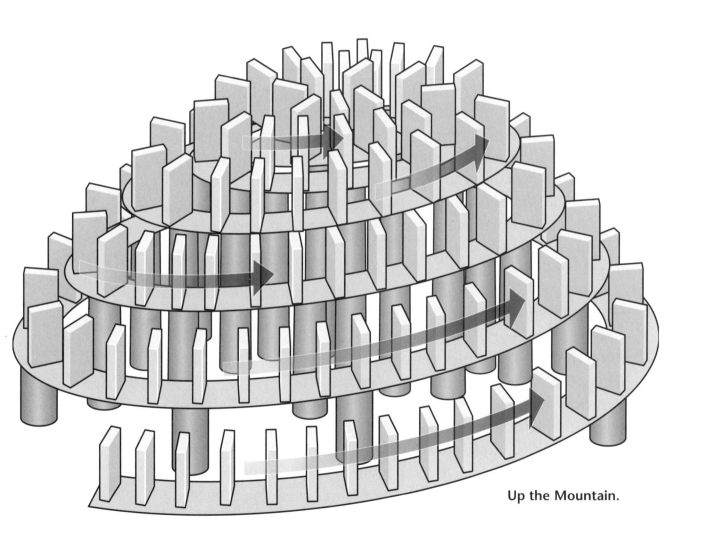

**Up the Mountain.**

# Some Concluding Advice

THE number of designs and tricks you can create with dominoes is limited only by your imagination. Some enticing ideas include strategically placing a nail through a hole in a domino so that it can run over tracks, like a toy train, or making loop-the-loops and other configurations, in which the domino is kept on the loop by centripetal force. Another is to have dominoes with metallic musical attachments that, when knocked over, play music. An entire formation can be designed to play a song.

Dominoes can also be painted one color on one side and a different color on the other side, so that as they fall they "reveal" a picture or logo that could not be seen before the dominoes toppled. This takes a tremendous amount of time, but is worth it for that special friend or client. I have created one setup in which the face of Benjamin Franklin was revealed.

The concept behind domino-toppling is simple: The very first domino is placed almost next to the thousandth—or ten thousandth, or hundred thousandth—so that all the dominoes will fall in a pattern. The trick is to make that pattern as interesting as possible.

Before you decide to demonstrate your domino-toppling skills to your friends or to TV cameras, there are some things you should be aware of: first, make sure of your surface. Never, *never* set up your dominoes on a rug. Second, it's not the jokers who knock over your domino formations, but some well-meaning schlemiel (Yiddish for someone who bends over in a restaurant to tie his shoe and has an entire tray of soup spilled on him). I've had to duck cameramen with long wires trying to get close-ups of my designs, carpenters on television sets who dropped nails onto the dominoes, and hundreds of other hazards.

If shouting "Look out" doesn't work, you may have to employ what I call a firebreak, a tactic that resembles one used by forest rangers fighting a fire. In a firebreak, I purposely leave out three dominoes for every hundred, so if someone or something triggers the dominoes accidentally, the chain will die out at the firebreak. Without this precaution, you'd be jumping all over the place trying to stop the chain, more often than not knocking over another line and causing more damage. With a properly placed firebreak, you should lose, at most, 100 to 150 dominoes. When you've become proficient and agile enough, you can make your firebreaks every thousandth domino and hope that you can get ahead of the inadvertently triggered line fast enough to knock out a few key dominoes and stop the damage.

What about picking up the dominoes after they've been knocked down? There are several approaches, including scooping them up with your hands, shoveling them up, and pushing them back into boxes with tools. The best, I've found, is to merely scoop them by hand. This somewhat primitive technique allows you to pick up about 2,000 in 15 minutes. With the other methods you may chip some of the dominoes, and that could be detrimental to your next setup because the damaged dominoes may fall prematurely or fail to strike the others correctly.

Now that you've mastered my tricks and designs, I look forward not only to hearing from you with any new concepts and contraptions you've devised, but also to seeing you in a head-to-head confrontation for the world record.

# Index